Hello, Family Members,

Learning to read is one of the most ~~~~~~~~ of early childhood. **Hello Reader!** ~~~~~ ~~ children become skilled readers who like to read. Beginning readers learn to read by remembering frequently used words like "the," "is," and "and"; by using phonics skills to decode new words; and by interpreting picture and text clues. These books provide both the stories children enjoy and the structure they need to read fluently and independently. Here are suggestions for helping your child *before*, *during*, and *after* reading:

Before

- Look at the cover and pictures and have your child predict what the story is about.
- Read the story to your child.
- Encourage your child to chime in with familiar words and phrases.
- Echo read with your child by reading a line first and having your child read it after you do.

During

- Have your child think about a word he or she does not recognize right away. Provide hints such as "Let's see if we know the sounds" and "Have we read other words like this one?"
- Encourage your child to use phonics skills to sound out new words.
- Provide the word for your child when more assistance is needed so that he or she does not struggle and the experience of reading with you is a positive one.
- Encourage your child to have fun by reading with a lot of expression . . . like an actor!

After

- Have your child keep lists of interesting and favorite words.
- Encourage your child to read the books over and over again. Have him or her read to brothers, sisters, grandparents, and even teddy bears. Repeated readings develop confidence in young readers.
- Talk about the stories. Ask and answer questions. Share ideas about the funniest and most interesting characters and events in the stories.

I do hope that you and your child enjoy this book.

—Francie Alexander
Reading Specialist,
Scholastic's Learning Ventures

For Alaina, Eric, and Brent
— F.R.

To all the little frogs of the world and the wonder of their diversity
— J.C.

Text copyright © 1999 by Fay Robinson.
Illustrations copyright © 1999 by Jean Cassels.
All rights reserved. Published by Scholastic Inc.
SCHOLASTIC, HELLO READER! and CARTWHEEL BOOKS and associated
logos are trademarks and/or registered trademarks of Scholastic Inc.

Library of Congress Cataloging-in-Publication Data
Robinson, Fay.
Fantastic frogs / by Fay Robinson; illustrated by Jean Cassels.
p. cm. — (Hello reader! Science Level 2)
"Cartwheel books."
Summary: Introduces the growth, food, habitats, colors, and shapes of different
kinds of frogs.
ISBN 0-590-52269-8
1. Frogs—Juvenile literature. [1. Frogs.] I. Cassels, Jean, ill.
II. Title. III. Series.
QL668.E2R535   1999
597.8'9—dc21   98-22398
                                                        CIP
                                                         AC
12 11 10 9 8   0/0 01 02 03 04

Printed in the U.S.A.   24
First printing, March 1999

Fantastic Frogs!

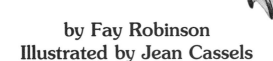

by Fay Robinson
Illustrated by Jean Cassels

Hello Reader! Science — Level 2

SCHOLASTIC INC.

New York Toronto London Auckland Sydney

Leaping over streams and logs.

Hip, hop!
Plip, plop!
Flip, flop frogs!

Short, squat bodies,
bulging eyes —
tiny frogs

or football-sized.

Maybe all the frogs
you've seen
are brown like bark
or leafy green.

But in the jungles far away,
frogs put on a great display...

Green or turquoise
poured on black.

Frogs with paintings
on their backs.

11

Racing stripes and
bold pink bellies.

Bright red frogs like berry jelly.

Frogs like sunshine,
glowing bright.

Others blue and black as night.

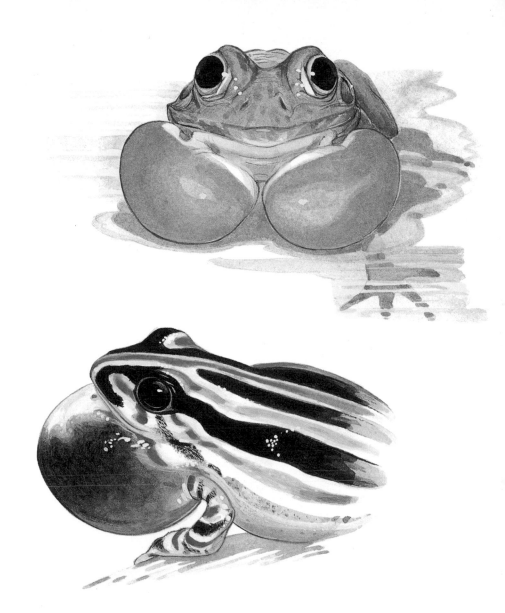

Chins blow out
like round balloons,
helping males sing
froggy tunes.

Eggs in gobs,

or eggs in rows.

Inside each egg,
a tadpole grows.

Tadpoles hatching
from their eggs.
They swim like fish.
They have no legs!

Back legs, front legs
start to sprout.

Soon a froglet hops about!

Frogs that climb.

And frogs that swim.

Frogs that fly.

And frogs that grin.

Bugs for lunch are very nice.

Big-mouth frogs might
dine on mice.

Bathing in the sun for hours.

Peering out of little flowers.

Eyes with hoods

and droopy folds.

Eyes like fire,

eyes like gold.

Silly frogs in funny poses.

Lumpy frogs with
big, long noses.

Leaping over streams and logs.

Hip, hop!
Plip, plop!
Flip, flop frogs!

Cover:
Red-Eyed Tree Frog

Page 6:
Goliath Frog

Page 12:
Red-Eyed Tree Frog

Page 4:
Bullfrog

Page 7:
Barking Tree Frog

Page 12:
Harlequin Frog

Page 5:
Bullfrog

Page 10:
Dart-Poison Frog

Page 13:
Strawberry
Dart-Poison Frog

Page 6:
Pygmy Banana Frog

Page 11:
Dart-Poison Frog

Page 14:
Golden Mantella

Page 14:
Blue Dart-Poison Frog

Page 19:
Froglet

Page 21:
Glass
Large-Eyed Frog

Page 15:
Male Short-Headed
Frog

Page 20:
White's Tree Frog

Page 22:
Green Frog

Page 15:
Male Painted
Reed Frog

Page 20:
Bullfrog

Page 22:
South American
Horned Frog

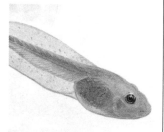

Page 17:
Tadpole

Page 21:
Asiatic Gliding Frog

Page 23:
Yellow-Spotted
Reed Frog

Page 23:
Dart Poison Frog

Page 25:
Malaysian
Red-Eyed Frog

Page 27:
Spatulate-Nosed
Tree Frog

Page 24:
Asian Leaf Frog

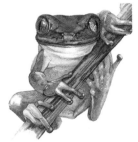

Page 25:
African Big-Eyed
Tree Frog

Page 28:
Leopard Frog

Page 24:
White's
Tree Frog

Page 26:
Red-Eyed
Tree Frog

Page 29:
Leopard Frogs

More Praise for *Sk*

"Longtime Savage readers, as v... ....
adoption memoir, *The Kid*, know how funny and ......
cantankerous he can be."

—*The Washington Post Book World*

"Full of acute observations and telling details."

—*The Dallas Morning News*

"A witty, irreverent, and thoughtful rebuke to conservative
culture critics like William Bennett and Robert Bork."

—*The Capital Times* (Madison, Wisconsin)

"A rhetorical smackdown of scolding guardians-of-virtue
such as Robert Bork and Bill Bennett . . . Funny and well
researched."   —*Orange County Weekly*

"Dan Savage is . . . a ranter of such fierce intelligence that
you enjoy his rash rush even when you disagree."

—*City Pages* (Minneapolis/St. Paul)

"A thoughtful look at our country's most common vices,
chock-full of facts and statistics . . . A great chance to laugh
at Savage as he laughs at himself and our national peccadillos."

—SFGate.com

Dan Savage is the author of the nationally syndicated column "Savage Love" and the editor of *The Stranger.* He is the
author of *Savage Love* and *The Kid* (both available from
Plume). He lives in Seattle, Washington.

most laugh-out-loud hilarious books of the year. But it's because *The Kid* doesn't remain a mere giggle-fest that it's also one of the best. Intelligent, provocative, and disarmingly honest, this is Savage's touching—and irreverent—love letter to his new son."
—*Entertainment Weekly* (named one of the Best Books of 1999)

"Savage tackles the politics of gay adoption head-on . . . Intelligent and honest . . . A love story, an argument, and a how-to book all in one."   —*San Francisco Chronicle*

"Gripping . . . engagingly readable . . . Savage has the slap-dash panache (and spot-on timing) of a stand-up comedian."
—*The Seattle Times*

Praise for *Savage Love*

"Gay or straight, readers lust for 'Savage Love.'"
—*Chicago Tribune*

"The American advice column has grown fangs."
—*The New York Times*